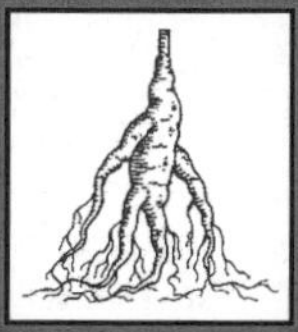

Humorous, visionary, and poignant alternative histories unfold in this collection of interlocking poetic narratives, which explore the lives of ordinary people in a small Wisconsin town. Each poem captures a unique perspective on the spiritual, mystical, and metaphorical world as the citizens of Merrill, WI try to make sense out of the mysteries and challenges of life.

Merrill
Springstead
LAC DU FLAMBEAU BAND OF LAKE SUPERIOR CHIPPEWA INDIANS
Lac du Flambeau
Crystal-Muskie
Star Lake
Sayner
Conover
Phelps
Nelma
Eagle River Union
Eagle River
Franklin Lake
Arbor Vitae
Wa-Swa-Goning
Emily L.
George W. Brown Jr. Ojibwe Mus.
Fishtrap
Woodruff
St. Germain
Snowmobile Hall of Fame and Mus.
Clearwater Lake
Sevenmile Lake
Minocqua
Three Lakes
CHEQUAMEGON NAT'L FOR.
Hazelhurst
Lake Tomahawk
Sugar Camp
McNaughton
ONEIDA
Hiles
PRICE
Willow Res.
Rhinelander-Oneida Co.
Logging Mus.
Starks
Argonne
Rhinelander
Woodboro
Crandon
Brantwood
Heafford Junction
Monico
Prentice
Tripoli
Bradley
Pelican Lake
Jennings
SOKAOGON CHIPPEWA COMMUNITY
Timms Hill 1951 ft. Highest Pt. in Wis.
Tomahawk
Harrison
Enterprise
Post Lake
Mole Lake
Spirit
Elcho
LINCOLN
Parrish
Summit Lake
Wisconsin
Irma
Perschon
Rib Lake
Gleason
Kempster
LANGLADE
Bloomville
Prairie
Whittlesey
Doering
Deerbrook
Bryant
Council Grounds S.P.
Polar
Goodrich
Antigo
Elton
Medford
Hamburg
Stetsonville
Elmhurst
Phlox
MARATHON
Brokaw
Big Rib
Athens
Little Chicago
Aniwa
Mattoon
Milan
Granite Peak
Eau Claire
Abbotsford
Wausau
Birnamwood
Schofield
Cherokee
Edgar
Marathon
Weston
Ringle
Hatley
Eland
Bowler
Rib Mtn.
Rib Mtn. S.P. 1924 ft.
Rothschild
Norrie
Wittenberg
Unity
Fenwood
Kronenwetter
SHAWANO
Tilleda
Eau Pleine
Halder
Mosinee
Elderon
Leopolis
Stratford
Bevent
Rozellville
Central Wis.
Knowlton
Tigerton
Split Rock
Galloway
Marshfield
Dancy
Marion
Marshfield Mun.
Hewitt
Rosholt
Little Wolf
Blenker
Milladore
Univ. of Wis.-Stevens Point
Bakerville
Auburndale
Park Ridge
Polonia
Peru
Big Falls
WAUPACA
Sherry
Junction City
Lindsey
Arpin
Stevens Point
Stevens Point Mun.
Custer
Iola
Bethel
Rudolph
Whiting
Nelsonville
Vesper
Arnott
Amherst Jct.
Scandinavia
Amherst
Pittsville
Wisconsin Rapids
Plover
Standing Rocks
Ogdensburg
Royalton
WOOD
Biron
Waupaca

the collection of Unintended Sutras

21 MEMORY PALACES

DONNA CAREY

DEVACHAN PRESS

DEVACHAN PRESS | VADITO, NEW MEXICO

Design: Sande McDaniel
Editor: Ariel Franklin-Hudson

Printer: Versa Press

This publication meets the minimum requirements of the
American National Standard for Information Sciences—
Permanence of Paper for Printed Library Materials,
ANSI Z39.48-1992. The paper is acid-free and lignin-free.

First Edition

Manufactured in USA

ISBN: 978-0-9716091-6-7
Library of Congress
Control Number: 2012932228

To my sister and brothers and their progeny.

To all my ancestors,
who live in and animate
the memory palaces of time.

To all people and alternative species—
friends, animals, plants, places—
who have helped me remember
the fugitive pieces inside the palaces
waiting to be pried open.

Contents

Unintended Sutras

Unintended Sutras

1

MEMORY PALACE

Holy Sonnet

for my nephew Nolan,

FROM C. VOYANT'S NOTEBOOK ON *ALTERATIVE ORIGINS* OF SPECIES, MERRILL, WI.

All penguins are listening,
swimming in water wisdom's
magnetic memory;
mutable imprints of freedom flowing.

we are talking creatures
resistant creatures

Animals have their own libraries of syllables,
harmonic alphabets, breath—
liquid language of inscape's rhyme,
transcendent ideograms,
pictographic telling of time.

we are talking creatures
caged creatures

Species and continents:
supernovas intend eternity's resonance,
birthing fragments of nebula's certain non-end,
pushing space's blankness
into sonnets of utter holiness.

we are talking creatures
searching creatures

Unintended Sutras

2

MEMORY PALACE

For the Time Being

the self arrays itself
forming the entire universe

Rivers and streams of stars
running into vast glades—
setting sun, risings tides,
fescue grass.

I am the reflection
of the glass that sets birds in a manger—
passing tides with perfect
strangers' nests,
exchanging mud and strings.

the self arrays itself
forming the entire universe
connection of things
entangled

We share a navel,
a single hole:
face of forever
tying us to stands that have held,
each to each;
folding into what we
hoped fed our hands
hands that
require our touching something,
evading grasp.

For the time being
mind does not think
or gut seize when it knows
what head does not,
what heart ignores.

Time is a moment
in any universe's day,
any speck within it is time
in suspended creation—
what the first atom dropped,
and where the circling went
from there to here.

Time in ratios and cones,
apprehended by souls' re-arrival:
subtract the tallies of sacred
tribal misgivings; add the
living, breathing escape-hatches;
tomorrow's additions are root numbers—
figure us in, despite our reluctance;
figure us in the formation
of dust and iceballs, tilts and reversals.

the self arrays itself
forming the entire universe

The self sends itself
into a pocket,
fumbling for change:
not what is missing
but what is learned
in spaces of new education;
currency earned
for the time being.

Remember us.

Remember when
we held dryer lint
in our beaks,
hair in our cheeks,
dug a garden by hand
in a heaving nuance,
and set out to make a home
from the distant alliances
of new songs bursting.

Unintended Sutras

3

MEMORY PALACE

My Gouda, Your Buddha

JERRY HOFFMAN,
CHEESE MAKER AND
TEMPLE PRIEST,
MERRILL, WI.

In Wisconsin
deep homage was paid.

An immense chunk of cheese
was placed on a throne,
paraded across the country
in a refrigerated truck.
(Forty days.)

In Wisconsin
deep homage was paid.

Many worshipped—
not only the thing itself,
but its time of becoming,
the maturity brine brings.
And many worshipped,
tasted this sublime piece of
heaven on earth.

Great was magic,
equalled to the non-equalled
weighing of fat and that thing
microorganisms conspire to construct
for spiritual pharmacology.
Soon its form became emptiness.

In Wisconsin
deep homage was paid.

Perfection in eight thousand slices.

Unintended Sutras

MEMORY PALACE

4

Friday Nights at the Green Lantern

Incantations always inspire us
to move beyond
conceptual categories.

Friday Fish Fry: All You Care to Eat

Lightly battered lake perch
Steak fries
Cole slaw you can't beat
Bavarian rye on the side

These sacred words were
uttered to the waitress, many
times round the table, and then
the addition:

Pitchers of brew on tap,
sports games, global map
the size of a poker table:
Where is there?

Platters came stacked and steaming,
each mouthful otherworldy,
and the transporting motion
of the ale so clear.

Country music
with accordion solos,
darts reaching the bull's eye
of the dartboard universe;
young and old stepping
on the planks to dance
into a wild ocean that seemed so vast
that cultivating corn,
and tabernacles, and children
was more than boring.

Tonight is the night
indivisible fabrics become real.

Offerings of land, sea, and sky;
Friday night fish fry
at the Green Lantern.
The potential so high that marriages
and so many other unions
seem salvageable.

I have come to understand as so many others

(in the dance hall), the meaning of fullness and emptiness.

Unintended Sutras

MEMORY PALACE

5

Dharmology

Every evening I can remember
our dad left the trailer
to work his second job
for noble truths.

We waited for him during
the mystic nights of summer vacation.
Running free all day,
we pressed leaves in waxed
paper, learned survival
from animals and flowers,
played baseball in the unkempt fields
where brambles of strawberries went wild.

At night we became a different species:
listeners to small and large vehicles,
cars and trucks,
speeding past on the freeway
that encroached our neighbourhood,
our trees, our solitude, our paths.
We waited, silent.

ALL SOUND IS NO SOUND
NO SOUND IS ALL SOUND

A motor: he has arrived
with expired food from
hospital vending machines:
potato chips, corn curls, pastries—

SENSATION AND PERCEPTION
PERCEPTION AND SENSATION

—bags that heal all suffering,
and we so full of desire for grease
that turns the wheels of time.
The glory of expiration dates.

He entered the gate and turned it,
then set to wash his hands.

The large bags he came bearing
sprouted into even larger bags
that took over the entire city,
fed the poor, blocked vehicle noise,
disrupted traffic on the freeway near our trailer
where a large lotus flower still blooms.

The four of us
now run a shrine,
charge admission to
see the miracle,
and keep the
vending machines
well-stocked.

Unintended Sutras

MEMORY PALACE

6

Holy Hands, Holy Cows

"DON'T EVER WEAR GLOVES FINISH WHAT YOU SET MOVIN'. HONOR EVERYTHING THAT CAN RESPOND TO YA, NO MATTER WHAT."

— PSALM OF MANNY PODALSKY, DAIRY FARMER, MERRILL, WI

I once read of a woman
who raised fowl for a special
feastday called Thanksgiving:
she gave the birds a big swallow
of Wild Turkey whiskey
before she slit their throats.

Now that is what I call compassion.

And I heard they gave those
young kids in the military,
just graduated from high school,
special gloves, so when they fought
in freezing temperatures,
at the front lines, the trigger finger
could be flexible and functional.
Problem is they got frostbite
in their feet and toes and died.

Now that is what I call compassion.

In the Sutras
(the intended ones that King James
and others
wrote)
there is a lot of
slight of hand:

Grasping, groping,
realms of myth and religion,
not real things that happen to
real people like dairy farmers
and ordinary folk from Wisconsin,
who end up on this long journey
of time—god knows where—
sometimes places they can't
even pronounce,
and nobody always has the
whole picture, nor should.

A phrase like "escape from the wheel"
means little to anyone taught
to "hold on to the wheel,"
or at best, it's congratulations for
trade-in on a vehicle past its usefulness.
Mostly, hands-down, escape's not an option
(same way changing jobs isn't
when your rent is covered)
to those who have climbed the highest mountain,
like learning to love their family of origin.

Now that is what I call compassion.

Hands are everything.
You can't drive a tractor,
throw hay bales, give a haircut
(although it's been attempted,
see for yourself by coming to town),
or signal a timeout if you coach football,
or gesture for a check at a restaurant
requiring shirts and shoes.
When you put someone to work
you don't call them a "hired foot."

Most of all,
we need hands for that special
dairy rite, something we call a moodra.
It is the act of dexterous hand movement,
the act of milking a cow—our most
sacred and precious friends
in this realm, the ones we count on.
Sure we all know life is suffering,
but there'd be a heck of a lot more
if not for milk and those beautiful creatures.

When we get ideas, when plans or
great crops come, when our kid gets voted
Student Counsel President or gets a free
fish fry at the Green Lantern for good grades,
when we bowl a golden game,
when our spouse pays us real good attention,
we press the fingers on our hands together
and say, "Holy Cow!" and really mean it,
Mean it with our hearts and stomachs
and everything else:

HOLY COW.

Unintended Sutras

MEMORY PALACE

7

The Way Things Appear

CONSTRUCTED FROM
THE DIARIES OF
EMMIT RAY, BEADMAKER
IN MERRILL, WI.

It wasn't the loss of his job
that worried him.

Give attainment up
to a great river
of non-attainment,
he was told.

Yes—that great body of water
called impermanence,
big 'ol river flowing free as boilermakers
on Friday night at the Green Lantern.

With so much time on his hands,
he thought he better use them.
He made strings of prayer beads
from gooseberries, but
friends told him point blank:

"You Duppa, Emmit!
Unless alternative rosaries
are fashioned from dingleberries,
caramels cannot run full circle."

Another friend sourced the word
"dingleberry". It wasn't in the
set of encyclopaedias he bought
from Claire, a college student neighbor
who helped shovel snow in winter
and weed in all the other months.

In the wiki-dictionary at Monroe County Library,
Claire was able to locate a remote connection
between the dingleberry and the barberry.
Everybody rejoiced at the Green Lantern,
understanding how all things connect.
(Claire later found her error:
it was really bearberry.
She never told a soul.)

On Friday night, when the last name
"Voyant" was called for a fish fry carryout,
Claire came to the counter to pick up her order.

Acquaintances gathered round,
raised her up above their heads,
declared, "You know everything, Claire!"
But Claire in her humility said,
"I don't know everything, but I do
know a few things about the dingleberry."

Blessed be the dingleberry.

Claire went on to master in botany
and write her thesis on the
cultivation of dingleberries in Midwestern climates.
She become an international scholar,
most famous for her book,
Bible of Dwarf Shrubs: Is it a Dingle or a Bear?
Dingleberries became famous at the
Green Lantern, and every Friday
they were served in all mixed drinks.
(The mayor banned maraschino cherries,
olives, and baby onions.)

Emmit recited his prayer beads 33 times.
Why? Because he had 33 living relatives,
counting next next of kin, and there are
33 geometries in the Shriyantra
He did a few extra rounds
because he heard on an
educational television show
that unless you hear something 80 times
remembrance is highly unlikely.
Claire confirmed this by email,
since she was away on her book-signing tour.

He recited night and day,
many things he did not understand.
Why? He was told by the berries themselves.

Listen to the words of the dingle.

And so he did.

Emmit became a kind of prophet—
you could say—
he opened a metaphysical store
where he sold dingleberry prayer beads
and rosaries.

Dingleberry prayer beads became so popular
that Claire worked on weekends,
helping to string, and invented a new technique
called string theory, whereby the work she did
on one bead could effect the others.
Claire also performed rituals she learned in Tibet
while lecturing on the compatibility matrix
of the common dingleberry.

Blessed be the common dingleberry.

Emmit felt things were not complete,
and began selling taffy apples seasonally,
so that caramels could run full circle.

And finally—

The world's largest stuppa was constructed
in Merrill City Center and dedicated to Emmit
with the tribute:

"To all those with vision
for a more fruitful tomorrow."

Blessed be the dingleberry.

And so it was.

Unintended Sutras

MEMORY PALACE

8

Tilt in the Dance Floor

We eat from a certain perspective:
our dinner table, the tilt in the planet.
Sometimes a tilt in what we feel
may be our sympathy for Earth,
the mystery of seasons, cycles of precession.
Sometimes the tilt is from bad carpentry,
so we shove in a shim to counteract the effect
not the cause—
but who can say what came first.

Are we circling around some big black hole?
Are we tilting?

Once I thought I was tilting
and took a level to my kitchen.
Turned out my left leg was shorter than my right.
Health insurance didn't cover that;
a chiropractor not only made me taller,
but gave me a lift in my shoes
and cracked me in ways I can't explain,
hooked up all kinds of connections.

Walking funny gave me new insights,
made me look further
into how each person sees and feels and tolerates,
just like how each person responds to sugars and proteins,
carbohydrates, new physics,
even the geology we stand on.
Things that align us:
our makeup, our mantle
cover-ups of all kinds, real history of rocks,
and a darn good waterproof mascara.

"Towns have markers, just like genetics,
places that orient them,
and those taking refuge in them,
constructing life and futures,
creating new generations within their fabric;
call it ecology of place, the sensitivity of a landscape,
pure tones of a breathing building
with a history and an ancestry, smells and laments.
Sometimes all we can do is shake our heads and grunt."[1]

[1] *Voyant, Claire. Alternative Origins of Species.*

Merrill has the Green Lantern
and Voyant's Botanical Gardens,
Scooter's Paper Mill (where we say
their environmental practices are pulp fiction),
and the Venturas' Bakery,
named after the only Filipino family in these parts.
The children, grandchildren and great-grandchildren
were straight-A students, and on occasion,
to keep community strong
and appreciate a .075% minority,
the Green Lantern serves tilapia
in coconut milk as a tribute to diversity.

Mostly, our hearts are a tilting point
that we try to straighten—but it keeps yanking.
Our planet shares that strange code, called geometry.
Some call this relationship
sympathy, others synchronicity.

Others call it nothing at all.

"The chambers in our heart slant at 23.1 degrees,
the same slant as our planet, Earth.
That is either some profound coincidence,
or a very meaningful chance event.
Not to freak you out, but the tilt of the dance floor
at the Green Lantern is at the same angle:
precisely 23.1 degrees."[2]

[2]*Voyant, Claire. Sacred Geometry, Sacred Geology,*
Sacred Physiology: Studies on Plants, Planets, and Us.

In Central and Northern Wisconsin,
a lot of Copper mine shafts are still in play:
the winding corridors of up and down and around.
Many things are whirling,
and there is pride in standing up
on your own two feet
upon a surface that is sea level (for now).
Removing minerals is always a dangerous balance,
so many folks have this ear thing,
and we just keep dancing,
dizzy with not only the symptoms but their cause:
this strange sense of tilting.

Swing your counterpart,
and pray the inner ear is intact.
Merrill is a cluster city for what experts call
Meniere's disease, an inner ear thing
Miners have a high incidence
of this syndrome as well—
that is why spelling
(the forming of words by ordering letters)
is so critical.

In appreciation for all those in Merrill
who suffer from balance trouble,
the Audubon society made a labyrinth
in the forest preserve,
near some serpent burial mounds.

Many say Merrill has strange electromagnetics
that effect humans and the migration patterns of birds—
kind of like the Horicon Marsh in Horicon, WI:
a 32,000-acre freshwater cattail marsh,
significant for its nests and the migration of
Canadian geese and many other species.
Stand in the vastness of wingbeats and mating calls,
the magnificence of burnt golds and rusts,
sounds of reeds slashing and cutting—
you open like a giant bankroll;
you become dizzy not just from the day
or the sun or the ephemeral beauty,
but from the reality of inflation.

At the Green Lantern, Claire Voyant
gave a special holiday presentation called
"Nativity, naivety, and how the manger
became an archetype and symbol
for future nests of the Midwest's aviary pantheon
and the berries they eat."
(I know you are wondering how this all connects.)

Claire's presentation was heavily attended
since everybody got 10% off Friday Fish Fries
and any drink purchases.
There was tremendous excitement
when folks heard it would be a MacIntosh
presentation! They brought caramels, nuts,
and Peppermint Schnapps to go with the apples.
People seemed to connect with some energy;
they were whirling.

Claire's contention
was that birds would be our saving grace,
because they follow magnetic poles, flipped or tilted.
Birds will show us how to orient ourselves
how to soar. They don't get dizzy
'cause they don't have ears with pretzels in them,
only holes with flaps to achieve astounding
aerodynamic balance and hearing.

"Many of the ancient cultures
along the Mississippi made bird mounds,
or crosses between birds and mammals—
strange breeds. They call them serpent mounds.
A few of these serpent mounds were found in Merrill,
(and came under a lot of scrutiny from archaeologists,
local Christians, and geneticists),
Wisconsin's very own Quetzalcoatl—
a new-fangled family of origin.
Information has been suppressed,
since birds and serpents represent a new time
of uniting with great energies,
in which the human field and the
bio fields of our planet and beyond
interact with a kind of synchronicity."[3]

The plot thickens now.

Some mounds are located at a 23.1 degree axis
from Milwaukee—
the same degree as the heart and the Earth are tilted,
and also the dance floor at the Green Lantern.
Some say there is a sacred geometry,
which is why some guidebooks
nickname it the "Shri-Lantern" and say
its dance floor spirals internally and externally.
It is why llama farms are so abundant in this area (Area 53),
so much akin to DNA.
Similar patterns have been found in crop circles in England:
when people enter they hear music and begin to get dizzy.

[3]*Voyant, Claire. Alternative Origins of Species.*

Here in Merrill, we say that planting crops is circular enough,
and the dance floor at the Green Lantern
carries generations of kin, and that is DNA.
If you don't get dizzy from the drinks,
the dance floor will kill you.

Claire invented a mixer called "Chutes and Ladders,"
added "Don't it Make My Brown Eyes Blue"
to the juke box selection,
and institutionalized scrabble
as the game of choice after dancing,
to raise language skills and help people
understand what mixing is about—
chance blends of an alphabet soup.
Though a botanist at heart, Claire minored
in molecular biology, and took a fancy to genetics.
She always said the Green Lantern was
a kind of stem cell or a cell tower.

She believed in Mendelian laws:
how we inherit things from small to large.
She gave a lecture at the Merrill Public Library
introducing the First and Second Laws of Genetics
in ways people could fathom:

"First is Merrill's law, the First Law of Mendel,
the law of segregation.
Next is Milwaukee and Chicago and Detroit's law,
the Second Law of Mendel,
the law of independent assortment.
More people, more possibilities, simple as that.
New laws are on the horizon:
look to the birds and eggs and flight patterns."[4]

[4] *Voyant, Claire. New Spins on Old Genes.*

Claire also believed in epigenetics:
she said we could change our thoughts, our minds,
change our DNA by what we think and dare to imagine.
The folks in Merrill followed Claire's philosophies:
think tanks developed at the Green Lantern,
next to the brewery
and pretty soon the town was full tilt,
so was its history and political membership
this town and all its inhabitants,
who changed how a small Midwest atoll
was viewed on the outside and the inside.

"Never underestimate the power of a few strange birds.
Keep your eye on all patterns, especially your own,
and other songs of self-creation. Mounds and sounds:
hearing is clearing, spinning is winning,
and spirals are milestones in the unknown reaches
of universes and tangles, from magnetics to epigenetics,
Tilapia to Utopia. Origins are on the move,
and we must move with that pull and tilt."[5]

[5] *Voyant, Claire. Alternative Origins of Species.*

Unintended Sutras

MEMORY PALACE
PALACE

9

Polar Bears

FROM C. VOYANT'S NOTEBOOK ON ALTERATIVE ORIGINS OF SPECIES, MERRILL, WI.

"Yet he no doubt delights the eye
of other hippopotami."
—E.E. Cummings

It is New Years' Day.
Polar bears plunge into
the frigid waters of Lake Michigan,
lubricated and intoxicated.

Water is neither strong nor weak.

The great road of the Buddha is crumbling.
Humans large, white, and shivering,
rinsing away the year's energy:
missed possibilities,
regretted snippets.
In the end all are naked,
or in giant swim trunks and bikinis
with frozen strings and things.

Some beings see water as a jeweled ornament.

I have traveled from my small town
to Milwaukee to witness this ritual cleansing.
Hopes for new decades and millennia—
emergence of a new species—
the day that water speaks of water.

Water is the dragons' palace.

Merrill is landlocked, like Uruguay:
it lies on the Wisconsin River,
so folks from there understand
that when water solidifies
it can challenge a diamond in hardness,
and when it melts it can compete
with milk and cherry blossoms in gentility.
Workings of water, like anything else,
can be exclusively dead or alive
depending on causes and conditions.

Waters freedom depends not only on water.

A busload of locals from Merrill
journeyed to the lakefront in Milwaukee
early on New Years' Day
to pay homage to wise old polar bears,
and join company with those who run in flesh
on the first day of the new calendar.
Those from Merrill began a three-day
observance in preparation for the event:
they fasted on Friday
and the Green Lantern served fish all week,
because purification rites created excess perch.
By Monday, all were ready to jump
into baptismal waves.

The path of water runs upward and downward, and in all directions.

Claire calls this string theory:
catch one thing one place,
and pretty soon all relatives and relatedness
come running, trickle down to everything
like water does:
resolutions without solutions;
string and water are infinite.

It is said
that although water belongs
to states and to nations,
water really belongs
to people who love water.

The January Lake Michigan water in Wisconsin
belongs to all the polar bears
who enter its subzero mystery.

It is not that there is water in the world
but that there is a world in the water.

Unintended Sutras

MEMORY PALACE

10

Returning Home

WORDS OF BERNIE OLENECHEZK, VETERAN AND MATERNAL GRANDFATHER OF C. VOYANT, MERRILL, WI.

It doesn't matter.
Here we are, in the world of form,
discovering more particles that define us,
new norms for the 21st century.
Doors opened, blind to the new assembly,
ways we've not heard of,
and hardly even imagined.

Battles keep playing:
gods waging wars,
humans carrying banners.
Centuries of replay:
red ground tries to forget
the ignorance of proper burials,
the lost rites of passage for the young,
human compost and no prayers,
the wheel spinning,
accumulating time and essence,
stealing from us.

So many wounds,
scars deeply felt,
an eternal sky splatters sun
on our planet's pelt
Help us understand
that our home and our land,
everything we swallow and taste
is everything we can't erase.
We carry it in our bones,
our humanity
our circumference.

I want to be the explorer,
traveling new territory in the
Midwest city-states of tomorrow,
cartography based on deltas
and the expansion of inside worlds,
reaching out to forgotten things
that matter again.
Screw Marquette and Joliette.
We have to get new passageways
for the greater need,
not destruction based on greed
larger than us

I want to go to garlic festivals,
and taste all the rivers
and Door County cherries,
hear bluegrass and catch bass from
wild waters
except for Sunday, when I skip out
of mass and go to the Green Lantern's
learning seminars

I want to sit by the Mississippi
on the boundary with Minnesota,
where camaraderie grows,
county fairs and apple pies,
greatest bratwurst and Barvarian rye breads
dark rich beer in giant kegs
and courage strong
as wooden legs bending song
carrying us to new deltas

I want to feed the people
who live under bridges.
I want to eat corn that is not
genetically modified,
I want to eat butter to preserve
my pride in creation
I don't want to attend
any more funerals for our kids
killed in war, trying to expand
our boundaries like imperialists,
dying on soil that doesn't smell
like autumn pumpkins and harvests.

I want to see Merrill's
brain and heart trust of tomorrow
not in a body bag, or living dead
in sorrows arms
(fuck Marquette and Joliette
and fuck France and fuck Rome).
I want to see them flying safely,
see the angels coming home.

Unintended Sutras

11

MEMORY PALACE

If It Ain't Butter, Don't Even Think of Eating It

NOTES FROM THE CLANDESTINE MEMOIRS OF MYRTLE STAR, DAIRY FARMER AND POLITICAL ACTIVIST FOR PRESERVING THE INTEGRITY OF RURAL PEOPLE AND THEIR PRODUCTS, MERRILL, WI.

Now when I probe into my memory
for clandestine activities
first thing that comes to mind
is the state line—
a boundary that was real alright,
back when Wisconsin and Illinois
had aggressive border patrols.
My aunt Milly told me this was
the start of a slippery slope,
a long battle against dairy farmers—
some life-long battle, separating
fat from meat and redefining
saturation and color therapy.

All this was back when
smuggling rings were in their hay-day.
Smugglers tried to sneak oleo
into Wisconsin, the dairy state—
bootleggers set up just over
the dividing line between Wisconsin
and Illinois (on the Illinois side),
constructed warehouses for oleo,
liquor, smokes, fireworks,
and marriage certificates.
There was even a mock
Lake County Courthouse,
with an attached chapel,
priests in vestments and
vanilla wafers for communion.
The outdoor grottos were slick
and shiny from polishing,
orange-yellow surreal brilliance.
Margarines Finish is a thing to behold.

Waukegan, IL housed the greatest warehouses,
that stretched all along Lake Michigan
to their Chicago roots.
You see, for total success,
everything must come from an auspicious root;
it's the roots that determine the quality
and the essential nature of the fruit.

Why I bring this up:
those engaged in the sale
of illegal goods and substances,
not charging due tax,
saw themselves as bodhisattvas
(advocating a good root system,
healthy warehouses of ancestors)
and resolved to liberate all beings,
end suffering—suffering that comes
from being dumb to transcendent rules,
how to bend that theory, and
avoid government.

As Claire Voyant has taught us,
in her lectures on the Diamond Sutras
at Keewanis Club: neither time nor space
can constrain a bodhisattva's path.
They are mobile charities
without attachment
beyond normal rules.

History of Oleo Margarine: Part One

Collective wisdom of the late 19th-century Midwest
taught us many things about oleo-margarine,
including sale, restriction, and labeling.
The government put a hefty tax on oleo,
and bootleg-colored margarine
became commonplace, escalating demands.

Just leave it to anything
deemed "illegal" to draw masses;
this is the reason for the mock chapels
in Waukegan.

With the World Wars that would
dominate the 20th-century zeitgeist,
the consumption of margarine increased;
dairy products were mostly unobtainable,
rations strict in the areas closest to the fighting.
When you think of how all things connect:
the UK imported a lot of butter,
some came from Wisconsin, but
the rest from Australia and New Zealand.
Risks of submarine activity meant no butter,
no sharp cheddar, briskets, Bob Hope—
or any hope, for that matter

Lobbies between dairy and margarine
continued to spread their influence
in politics and mainstream,
lending and melting fat content,
until the public was emulsified,
and nobody knew what saturated
bonds were anymore
(except for lobbyists and economists).
The Depression helped pro-dairy;
Second World War swung back to margarine.

Waukegan is a Potawatomi word
meaning "trading post"—
it attracted settlers as a port city, a seed city.
It was on Lake Michigan,
vessels could come and go,
things could take root.
Later, when the Railroads were built,
it became a major manufacturing center:
more could come and go,
root and seed into a Midwest futura.

Waukegan became an epicenter of activity
for all kinds of intrigues:
high on the list of inequities
was the sale of oleo,
representing 80% of its economics,
and drawing much of the state of WI
into the mystery of "the other."

Once folks were down in Waukegan,
picking up their oleo and Marlboroughs,
hell, why not get married
or step into the casinos near the grotto?
Like my dear auntie said,
it was the start of a slippery slope
against the dairy farmers.

Little by little,
margarine restrictions were lifted:
Minnesota 1963, Wisconsin 1967.
Vestiges remain today:
ever see a pack of margarine
larger than a pound?
Thank the Food, Drug, and Cosmetics Act.
Yellow margarine remains illegal
in Missouri, as well as the packet of dye
you mix and squeeze into something
we cannot, refuse to pronounce.

In Merrill, we take pride in our roots, dairy farmers.
Though some take that tedious, guilty ride
over state lines, it is usually for other substances,
at super malls and amusement parks
that sprung up in Waukegan,
not for oleo margarine. We say:
"If it ain't butter, don't even think of eating it."
Waukegan certainly isn't for swimming:
It contains three sites of
hazardous substances that are on the
national priorities list. We say:
"If it ain't water don't even think of swimming in it."

Bad seeds, contaminated roots and groundwater,
more PCBs than DVDs, more landfills than bluegills,
more asbestos than fiestas—just what kind of fruit
can you produce from this root?
Ray Bradbury was born there
and wrote about his hometown:
Something Wicked This Way Comes, Farwell
Summer and other stories. Waukegan got
cleanup dollars and named a park after him.
Some couple wrote a novel called *Stardance*
that nobody read, about a prototype of planet Earth—
gravity versus free fall
could only be Waukegan.

History of Oleo Margarine: Part Two

In our brief time together
we cannot begin to tackle
things like the development of spreads,
manufacturing, co-mingling,
illicit marriages of oleo and butter,
politics of biochemistry,
market acceptance, debates on
fats saturated, unsaturated, and trans.
What we can provide are facts:
the facts tell us about brand marketing,
how commercial TV emphasized competition—
things changed in the '60s:
What tasted most like butter? Is it real?
A spread? A spy? What?

Margarine—especially polyunsaturated—
overtook butter consumption by the end
of the 20th century.
Margarine has a special market:
to those observing the Kashrut
mixing meat and dairy products
is a no-no, and margarine is the kosher choice.
The late 20th century underwent a Passover:
margarine shortage was met with
consternation in the Kosher community;
margarine is vegan—and most folks
don't know it was once made of meat.

We were once cannibals,
so little really changes.

HDL, LDL, PCBs, RVs,
saturated, unsaturated,
contamination, recovery—
where there is suspicion,
there is reason for asking,
where there is smoke, fire.
If you have to plant a seed,
where do you get the water?
Go to the source, the root
of what is unadulterated.

We dairy farmers
planted a holographic image in the soil
that Claire received in a dream
about the Milky Way:
golden drops rained down on
Wisconsin and Minnesota,
spilling into the rolling hills,
and the fields that farmers honor
with wolf moons and bowling.
Giant trees grew overnight,
bearing fruit of quarter-pound sticks
of glorious butter, sold in supermarkets
in super quantities.
Sales went off the charts,
butter was re-rooted in Midwest economy,
Waukegan wept.

History of Oleo Margarine: Part Three

Butter held its ground, eclipsing oleo
in the 21st century. Like eggs,
butter underwent a kind of redemption
in the gestalt of human health—
cholesterol and the things that
break it down and balance it
vs. sacrificing taste and fat
for known disappointments,
engineering flaws,
and future carcinogenic crises.

Red wine became to butter
what lecithin was to the egg yolk:
nature's liberation, delicate harmonies
not new to Europeans.
And as you can guess,
it wasn't long before Waukegan's
vineyards spread clear across all
Lake County, Illinois
and deep into the heart of Wisconsin.

Unintended Sutras

MEMORY PALACE

12

Remote Viewing

REPORTS OF THE PARANORMAL FROM LANCE MAINARD, 3RD GENERATION POLICE OFFICER, MERRILL, WI.

I was called to investigate
what we classify as a "breach in protocol"
at a floating casino on the Mississippi
that anchored overnight in Prairie du Sac.
See, gambling isn't legal in Wisconsin—
only on Indian lands or in bars run by mafia
on the East Side of Milwaukee—
so there are many Mississippi gambling cruises,
flotillas of slot machines, black jack, poker
and seven card hold 'em.

I will be the first to admit

that farmers are forever betting on the weather;
the Green Lantern hedges bets
on local fishing for Friday's business;
we all gamble on obtaining a spouse,
a family, a community, a job—
the one that comes up in the cards isn't always a keeper.
My grandma Emma Steward says, "You got to know
when to hold them and know when to fold them."
Manny Podalsky says, "Better to bend than break"

(There are many things beyond understanding.)

Well, what I was called to investigate
was beyond me, beyond what my training
on the force prepared me for.
Remote viewing is what they called it,
some kind of paranormal activity,
gathering information about distant targets,
an unseen method of employment—
in other words extra-sensory perception. ESP.

What in the world is a remote viewer?
Simply put, it is a viewer expected to give
accurate information about something
hidden from physical view,
and at some distance—
sometimes very great distances.
The viewer flies there in a different body,
the same body they actually have,
the spirit part flies and hooks onto the energy
of the thing it's looking for.

The government funded some
ESP research—the CIA, and then the
Air Force, and the most famous
results were when viewers discovered
a new class of Soviet submarine,
and a downed bomber in Africa.

I had some encounters with remote viewing
through an old girlfriend, Claire.
We still talk and have dinner together;
we have a very special bond
that nothing in the world can shake.
Like her mama, her skin is too thin—
maybe mine is too, though that is
not her opinion; she said I was thick as a brick,
thick as the frost in the marshes come December.
Huh, they say people develop greater understanding
and compassion as a side effect
of remote viewing.

Better not to compare things.

Anything, really, since in the process
we annihilate each thing's uniqueness.
Claire is certainly unique.
Sometimes we would pack snacks
and a cooler of ice cold beer,
lie under the willows,
watching the clouds move around the planet,
making secret codes—everything full
and smelling so grand, near perfect except
ambient tension in myself
for always feeling judged by her.
Deep down I have my own opinions, evaluations,
and assessments of myself. I trust myself.

Out of nowhere she would say:
"Hey Lancy, what do you say I check out
the daily specials at the Green Lantern?
How much you want to bet I can get them all right?"
Then she would go into a trance—
I got to know that look intimately, sense not feeling
of catching yourself falling and at the same time
understanding feelings and thoughts you are having
—and she proceeded to recite
the entire menu as if it were a concert, seeing different
in space and time, 3D/4D thought forms.

I recorded them, every special, entrée, a la carte, dessert,
not only bearing witness, an apostle to remote viewing,
but preserving the process in awe. You just have to create
different alternatives-
have to forgive and give up the need to be right,
to even up the score
have to know your inner landscapes.
What a day with spring flowing like
an ocean connecting all living things—
this is not guesswork, it is bending metals,
converting body matter to energy
for mental exertion.

Other times, Claire would "tune in"
to local movie theatres to view the listings,
and even watch a preview. This was a blessing,
since I could ask off in advance
and not cause scheduling conflicts at the station.
Every now and then she would check
the expiration dates that were not stamped
on packages from the food co-op:
she would go all the way back
to the growing process, the seeding,
the day things were produced.

Cool, but scary. I want her body in her body,
her mind back in her brain, not into shifting
patterns recruiting everything to become
the same thought.
When you know things in this way
it doesn't mean you have wisdom insight,
just a technology of mind, part of what happens
in this material world, a learned ability to sense
wave form data as though the world is only thought.

Maybe it is.

Claire had strict ethical codes for looking.
Though the temptation was always there,
she follows the codes—always has.
I suspect she always will.

The floating casino, named Enigma, was a major challenge.
I was summoned as an "expert," because I had been
on many paranormal cases, had a reputation
as a person of deep insight and intuition,
as well as someone who followed the letter of the law,
believed in the objectivity of science,
and the sanctity of investigative facts.
They called me a bridge.

Enigma casino was broke.
No money, no cash stores—
meaning somebody, or somebodies,
had won the house and put it in foreclosure.
They knew the codes, had used unusual means
to retrieve information—in-house cameras,
videos, security, and staff revealed
business as usual. No computer breaches,
no ordinary explanations.

Claire accepted my invitation to join me for an adventure.
Soon we were aboard the Enigma,
sloshing in a harbor many miles from Merrill
(having a fish fry on a Friday night).

We talked, caught up on life—
small things that make the heart feel good
and help you avoid the bigger things,
like the telepathy that occurs frequently
between people who are close for a long time—
separate parts of the universe connected
in an intimate way that influence one another
and allows growth to arrive
without effort

Days passed, and we began to suspect
it was a case of remote viewing, a perfect crime:
no fingerprints, no evidence on the scene,
just strange images in reverse,
imprints in the matrix.
Claire traced the images
back to East Side Milwaukee,
to a notorious gambling kingpin named Ricky Rodgers.
(With Claire you take the backseat—
fine with me.)

Ricky said he needed money
for his kids' college, that the Jesuits kept
raising tuition—why not arrest them for extortion?
Ricky hired a medium, who connected to the boat,
and viewed 360 degrees through a portal—
the same one Claire travelled back through—
saw cards and hands and decks, and
signalled everything back to headquarters.
The boat was cleaned of cash in minutes.

Claire and I talked all night long,
about the fine line between gifts and curses,
abilities and pretensions, talents used to destroy and create,
about distinctions, and what we ultimately want
to let into our field of view and belief.
We both missed each others' strangeness,
visible and invisible forces around one
another that have taught us to interact harmoniously
to believe in one another.

If I was granted one wish, just one,
I would wish for the ability to see into Claire's heart,
to find out, really see, what she needs.
When we were kids we shared everything;
we had an idyllic kind of friendship;
maybe I pushed too hard for more as we got older—
sometimes I just see, feel things that are right,
and respond to them.

I am a responder to accidents, deaths,
cats caught in trees, fellas beating their wives,
old ladies with pensions stealing washcloths from Walmart—
to all kind of crimes, rolling through stop signs,
rolling through life. Not just the physical stuff—
I hate things left undone and unfinished,
projects and relationships.

I hate the damage I see every day:
car wrecks and train wrecks of all sorts,
but nothing can compare to the human damage
that comes from not paying attention
to the things and people we love,
not paying attention to ourselves.

I pay attention more these days.
Claire has taught me that.
Maybe once I was thick, but I have
recognized, deep down, the thin lines
in others and myself—
lines drawn on us, before us, within us,
and the lines we trace ourselves,
lines between worlds and dimensions.
Ultimately life is a struggle
between belief and non-belief,
life's true drama and religion.

I will never be a hero,
chasing ghosts and looking into a future
that I do not have the courage to change.
I will never father children (yet I will be a father),
I will never marry (yet I will be a husband).
I believe in many things—apple blossoms in spring
floating dreams of generations, circularity of life,
my father.
I may not fully understand Claire
but I can bend to see things I have never seen.

I once read that Irish bards trained to become poets
for something like 30 years
lived in dark underground chambers,
memorizing histories, poetry, songs
people did not write back then, so the bards learned
rules of oral composition, learned to see in the dark.
Poetry and its chanting was the vehicle to take humans to
Tir no n'Og, the goddess inhabited island, the
many coloured land of realization where Claire lives sometimes.
I have been invited and visited
this land many times myself, carried on the poetry
of belief.

Even if we cannot understand or possess something,

we can still love it,

believe in it,

embrace it,

Close or at a distance.

Love it however we can, and that may allow
for unusual possibilities
alteration of heart
to bridge strange and daunting new worlds
we can burst into or
illuminate the one right here in front of us.

Unintended Sutras

MEMORY PALACE

13

Theories of Hypothermia

RECOLLECTIONS OF
RUTH ANNE JOHNSON,
PUBLIC LIBRARIAN,
MERRILL, WI.

In the old days
people believed
that if you kept your feet warm
the rest of the body would follow.
And sure, other theories came
to replace that one
but they left quickly
like new neighbors
from Southern California.

KEEP YOUR EARS WARM,
THE REST OF THE BODY WILL FOLLOW.
KEEP YOUR HANDS WARM,
THE REST OF THE BODY WILL FOLLOW.

There were antidotes for frozen hands,
like placing frozen digits under your armpits,
or down your pants or other people's pants.
And there were antidotes for frozen ears,
like listening to your husband or wife.

A particular theory that stayed for a long time
and actually proved itself credible was:
keep your neck warm
and the rest of the body will follow.

SINCE I WAS A BIBLIOPHILE,
AND HAD ACCESS TO HISTORY
AND MANY THEORIES ON HYPOTHERMIA,
I DID A TREMENDOUS AMOUNT OF RESEARCH,
AND FOUND THAT IN MANY CULTURES
THE NECK IS THE PLACE TO KEEP WARM AND COVERED.
IT KEEPS WHAT THEY CALL EXTERNAL PATHOGENS OR EVILS OUT.
CERTAIN ORIENTAL PHILOSOPHIES OF MEDICINE
HAVE FANCY NAMES FOR DIFFERENT PLACES,
CALLED "WIND GATE" AND "WIND PALACE"
SINCE WIND BRINGS THINGS IN—
THINGS YOU DON'T WANT.

Flip side is wind brings things
you do want, might want,
like seeds and weather,
storms and rain, possibilities
and change in general.

Anyway, makes sense in a way,
since the first thing you get
when cold penetrates
is a stiff neck and a sore throat.
Merrill responded to this theory
by inventing neck warmers.
The knitting stores ran knitting circles
to produce scarves and wraps,
and a kind of hybrid scarf and hood.
Merrill became an economic hub,
the most successful city
in this neck of the woods.

My granddaddy Hans von Hine was a visionary.
He believed that the most important
anatomical feature to keep warm
was the keister. Part of his rationale
was that folks celebrate Easter
with a smoked ham—a pig's keister—
so when you think of it,
the keister has always had a sacredness.
"Tradition is based on collective wisdom,"
was Hans' contention.
"Memories float through time and space
and congeal in a kind of local head cheese."

Hans was a contemplative man,
survivor of a world war like my father—
but it was said that his comrades
failed to cover his butt, and now
my daddy is dead and buried.
When a parent survives their child
there is remorse and grief same as when
a child survives their parent.
Grandpa had a mission after his son's death
and so did I.

Since he remembered so much history
of Merrill and elsewhere, remembered
the days of metal bar stools, before plastic
and imported goods and global economy,
remembered his son's demise—
one day he had an epiphany:

"IF YOU KEEP YOUR KEISTER COVERED
THE REST OF THE BODY WILL FOLLOW."

So Hans invented the keister cover,
a battery-operated device,
a sort of forerunner to the electric blanket,
placed directly inside the underwear.

Specificity is what I call it,
an itch to quell the scratch—
I forget the fancy French name for it,
but when a great need presents itself
something will surely come to fill it.

Grandpa became famous.
Folks all over the Midwest
bought keister covers for everything
from sitting on metal barstools,
to riding in cold trucks to check snow fences,
to cures for hemorrhoids.
The papers called it "The Midwest Jalapeno."

When the keister is warm
the rest of the body will follow.

Since there weren't things back then
like intellectual property laws
and patenting and such—
at least not for folks like us—
this concept caught on.
Grandpa's since passed on,
but he would be proud to know
that his invention influenced
the auto industry's heated seats
and Kundalini yoga
(if the root is not hot nothing will rise),
and far-reaching ideologies in corporate
America, and even worldwide.

Grandpa called his invention a "cryoprotectant,"
but in his simple words he said:

"IF YOU KEEP YOUR BUTT MOVING
YOU'LL STAY WARM AND AVOID HYPOTHERMIA,
AS A GENERAL RULE THOUGH,
IT IS ALWAYS BEST
TO COVER YOUR BUTT."

Unintended Sutras

MEMORY PALACE

14

All's Well that Bends Well

EMMA STEWARD
ON BAMBOO,
MERRILL, WI.

Ginseng farming isn't all it's cracked up to be.

The family got into it via Oriental relatives
—sister cities and such.
I suppose most of the businesses in America
got started that way: not by Europeans.

When tit comes to tat
ginseng will outlive bratwurst,
and the east will outlive the west—
same direction birth came from, sun rises.
Not that it's a competition.
All is well in the world,
and we all need to bend a bit,
set a new course of direction.

Ginseng is very unique.
looks like a person,
'cept it doesn't have tattoos or piercings.
Ginseng has arms that extend upwards to heaven,
feet planted on the Earth, rooted deep like
you and me as usual pulled in tension
between two extremes.

That's why I prefer bamboo:
one of the hardest substances
to break down or pull apart,
it can yield and bend, but doesn't break.
If only hearts were as strong —
hearts and backs.

Manufacturers in Merrill
have begun making flooring of bamboo;
bowls too, and wind chimes, cutting boards,
matting, rugs, fences
Green Lantern has a tiki bar made of bamboo,
the Buddhist monastery in Oregon, WI has
bamboo groves since they create a
peaceful and meditative setting, and the Shinto shrine
in Merrill has sacred objects made of bamboo—they say it is
a symbol of longevity

But ginseng made itself famous for raising stamina.
God knows we need all the help we can get
to boost energy in these tired days.
Ginseng requires fancy sheds and lots of watering;
it requires high maintenance, prayers, relationships—
like people.

Bamboo, you can let go free:
it sways and it stretches,
bends to eternity.
My friend Manny Podalsky once said,
when the big corporations
finally wore him down
and bought out his dairy farm,
"Better to bend then to break."

His granddaughter Claire
taught him about Eastern philosophy—
I would have said you got to know when
to hold 'em and know how to to fold 'em, like we do in cards,
poker and sheep's head.

Manny knew a lot about bamboo
from his early days of backyard gardening.
He staked up tomatoes with bamboo poles
and let the beans run up 'em,
used them like re-bar.
None of the stalks ever broke;
even woodpeckers couldn't make a dent in 'em.

Remembering this miracle from years since passed,
Manny began to grow bamboo on the acres he kept
from the farm sellout. He says bamboo's
one of the most long-lived perennials,
1,500-plus species flourish on this beautiful planet,
more than cows and ginseng put together.
Bamboo lives longer, too—
longer than least desirable in-laws.
Even though bamboo is native to China and Japan,
it's been growing here in Merrill forever.

Bamboo grows without pesticides, without fertilizers.
When you farm like Manny and me,
and most folks in Merrill,
that is most of the cost, hands down.
I have been growing ginseng for many years,
a family habit started in Michigan,
another Midwest state.

Ginseng's different.
First off, it's a root—a special one at that.
Once a plot of land has been used for ginseng
it can never be used again for ginseng.
Special beyond special, just not cost effective.
Ginseng lasts 3-6 years, like the perfect partnership—
except with ginseng, the older it gets,
the more human it looks.

My granddad grew the largest root ever, over 7 foot tall.
He told me a story once, of how it turned into a person,
walked into the credit union where he had his farm loan,
wrote a check and paid it off for him—
beyond special and very cost effective.

That is the reason we keep growing ginseng.

Claire says miracles repeat themselves
every second generation, like genetics.
Take diabetes for instance, or twins,
night blindness, the gift of vision.
I read all about this in Claire's
Alternative Origins of Species.
Claire's maternal grandpa, Manny Podalsky
said I should use the empty ginseng plots to cultivate bamboo
fill emptiness with fullness, expect miracles.
That way I can have it all.

Better to bend than to break.

Manny says I won't be sorry,
that he wouldn't give me a bum steer.
Ha! When we were dating he sold me an angus,
cranky old cow as full of grizzle as my ex-husband.
No thank you.

I planted anyway, and was never sorry.
Manny sells bamboo to the mills
along the Wisconsin River,
clear into Fox Valley and as far away as
Minnesota and Mexico—
for paper, flooring, thatch,
and musical instruments.

Bamboo is a completely renewable crop,
and since sustainability is popular now,
along with what they call eco-friendliness,
demands for bamboo to make clothing
for yoga and tai qi exceed supply.
That is where all my bamboo goes.

A very strange and fascinating phenomena
associated with plant life is bamboo
"mass flowering", where every
bamboo stock of the same flower-type
blossom at the same time every
50-60 years—
when the bamboo shoots flowers
it's the end of its life cycle
ca-poot
no matter their geographical location
Claire Voyant writes about mass extinction
in her book *Alternative Origin of Species*
comparing it to Christian rapture

The other day I took a nap—
unusual for me, but I fell asleep,
and dreamed that bamboo was being
used by the military, since it is hard as steel
(I am sure my research on bamboo was part of this).

*All of the cannons and guns, arterial
shells, swords, everything that ever looked
like a loaded phallus intended to harm—it
all shape-shifted through history, turned
into bamboo flutes that everybody on Earth
began to play in harmony.*

When I woke up the local credit union
the one I have my farm loan at
called to say a tall, sort of anthropomorphic
lookin' woman carrying a bamboo flute
wrote a check to pay off my loan.

Unintended Sutras

MEMORY PALACE

15

Ancestors

"You had better go back
and think it over again
for a couple of days
then submit to me another stanza."

— Hui-Neng

Claire's ancestors built a giant root cellar
made from a culvert (also used for road construction),
and stocked it full of all the food they grew and processed,
canned goods, root vegetables, honey, saltines, homebrew,
just in case there was another Cuban Missile crisis—
or at least to make it through the hard winter every year.
Folks back then were much more self-sufficient.

The funny thing about this root cellar
is that it was seldom used for its intended purpose,
to feed the living.
Instead, it attracted other forces: hungry spirits,
hungry for birth stories, to communicate secrets, to satisfy thirst,
spirits who wanted to relocate to Merrill
and didn't want to go through proper channels.
A spirit will always give more than it takes;
they left star charts, masks, jewels, pottery, poetry,
which is why the cellar kept expanding,
well beyond its physical capacity
It seemed like a portal that went on forever,
a wormhole through places with no maps or references—
a star gate of sorts.

There are caves like this in Bayfield, Wisconsin,
some in Blue Mounds, and some in the Apostle Islands.
In *Alternative Origins of Species*,
Claire talks a lot about the Apostle Islands,
about how apostles were pioneers, a new species.
The naming of the islands was not about how the missionaries
evangelized the Indians—not that they followed a historical Jesus
to conversion—but a kind of messenger archetype,
an image from way back that people share,
that lives in the caves of our unconscious, in clear water down deep.
Claire says it is not about conversion, but the conversion experience.

Carl Jung discovered the archetype in a dream about Neolithic caves.
The Red Book was about his encounters with the Indians
—written in code—through the opening that linked
the caves in Switzerland to the ones on the Apostle Islands.
The portals on the Islands sent spirit messages all over the world,
as far as Mexico, Mongolia, Egypt, and the Bahamas.

According to Claire, these caves may have been
how many new species arrived in Wisconsin,
ginseng and bamboo,
and things from other dimensions.

Claire's grandma told her the story of how Che Guevara
flew into the root cellar one day,
and was sitting on the bench eating her pickled asparagus,
guzzling choke cherry wine, nonchalantly smoking a cigar.
Next winter when she went down to fetch a jar of cling peaches
she found a box of hand-rolled cigars
and a red flag that said "Vive la Revolution."

Now and then people would come through—
and strange animals and insects, strange tools and rocks and flowers,
giant spiders that recited Carl Sandberg,
and chucks of Manchego cheeses from the Spanish Inquisition.
They ate and drank as they pleased—because journeying
long distances to tell a story works up an appetite.
Claire's great aunt said it was in the family, to be innkeepers,
to feed hungry travellers, to have an open-door policy.
Great Aunt Harriet owned a restaurant in Eagle, WI:
the Eagle Inn near Kettle Moraine, where geological features
from the last Columbian Ice Age could be observed.

One day a large woman sat down in the Eagle Inn,
and ordered a pitcher of Lienenkugel beer
and six iceberg lettuce super-salads with extra-croutons.
(This was nothing out of the ordinary for folks in Wisconsin.)
Harriet couldn't see too well, but when she put on her glasses,
she noticed the woman was a Wooly Mammoth,
and her kids were grazing in the backyard.
After the family had eaten all her columbines for dessert,
they left her some tusks, and permafrost to keep her beer extra cold.

Strange things happen when we keep our doors open.
All things operate according to patterns that are different at different times.
Some ancestors are transient phenomena destined to unravel,
others persist through sheer will, leaving clues and memory threads,
imprints for us to unwrap or camouflage.
Spirals of ancestry help us to reach disorder—though it itself is ordered.
It cradles us through the cellar until we rotate towards the opening,
independent of our collected contents.
Eventually we appear uniquely born out of nowhere
like ancestors who send their flags to live new revolutions.

"This was handed down and it is
not a system of my own invention
those who wish to hear the teaching
should each clear up their own doubts
the same way the sages did in the past."

—Hui-Neng

Unintended Sutras

MEMORY PALACE

16

Bowl-der-geist

A COMMUNAL EFFORT OF
THE MERRILL LANTERNS

Another Wednesday night
at Pinky's Bowl,
wearing retro sportswear,
golden like perfectly fried fish
with black sleeves and ribbing
over the front pocket,
for all the world to see
the logo of the Green Lantern Tavern:
a beckoning lantern,
green chain stitching underneath
spelling out "Merrill Lanterns."
This is Midwest simplicity,
straightforwardness you don't find
many places anymore.

There was a lot of hesitation,
even nervousness around finals
and hybrid teams coming in from
Milwaukee—triple-sponsored
with sparkling balls.
These teams were vicious,
had the right to be because
the only syndicated bowling show,
"Bowling for Dollars," was filmed
there at Bobbie Lanes, up the street
from where Laverne and Shirley
ate ice cream sundaes
and slurped Coca Colas.
The bowling show host
killed a person—he was DUI
and did time, but time snakes
back around on you,
lands you out of the cell
you put yourself in,
repent and repeat—scores
never really settled, not really.

A LOT WAS AT STAKE:
REPUTATION, TERRITORIES
IMPORTANT TO DEFEND
IN A MIND AND IN AN ALLEY—
ALMOST ANYWHERE A TEMPER
CAN FIND FUEL AND A SPARK.

In Merrill, even though
there was an unsettled air,
the Lanterns knew they
had a home field advantage.
They were favored
by the unseen world—
an incredible world,
deciding affairs and competitions.
Claire called the inhabitants
of this special world
the "Bowl-der-geists,"
said it was good
to have friends in high places
making sure you didn't
get foot fungus from rental shoes
and were able to pull off
a legal strike if you intended.

More importantly,
these friends helped to
honor the principles
of guests and hosts,
maintaining equilibrium
between seated and non,
spare and sparing—
seating is everything
to be spared is everything.

Bowl-der-geists were socialists
(or more correctly,
believed that socialism
must have democracy to back it up)
Bowl-der-geists rooted
for the common man,
didn't drink fancy-ass beers
brewed in small quantities;
they emptied glasses of
Pabst Blue Ribbon,
read Leon Trotsky,
Between Red and White,
Literature and Revolution, and
Their Morals and Ours—
you couldn't find one Trotsky book
left on the Merrill library shelf,
nor anything on Marxism.

THE FOLLOWING IS QUITE CLEAR:
1) NOBODY CHECKED THE BOOKS OUT.
2) THERE WASN'T A RECENT BOOK BURNING
3) THE CHRISTIANS DIDN'T STEAL THEM.
4) AGATHA CHRISTIE DID NOT EAT THEM.

That leaves our non-material friends.
Non-materialism is exactly what
they have in common with Trotsky.

Bowl-der-geists were drawn
to the bowling alleys
by the sound of thunder
and a desire to help
ordinary people understand
how the language of the sport
evolved, how it reflected the personal
(how the gods expressed themselves).
Avid readers, it seemed they left
a Trotsky book on the bar
at the Merrill Bowl
during a Lantern practice,
Lessons of October.

A particular sentence was lit up:

"THE FUNDAMENTAL INSTRUMENT OF PROLETARIAN REVOLUTION IS THE PARTY."

The Merrill Lanterns
were ecstatic with this proclamation
and increased intake of boilermakers
on Friday nights at the Green lantern
and at Pinky's Bowl while in training:

long live the party
and those in favor of it
thanks for all gifts
and every producing still
praise the gods
and all unseen and unsightly.

"Every period in the development of the party has
special features of its own and calls
for specific habits and methods of work."

Claire rallied the team:

**UNITE AND CONQUER THE MILWAUKEE KEGS!—INTENSE
SHOTS ARE NEEDED, LIKE THE HOOK
AND ABILITY FOR AGILITY OF SPLITS—LONG LIVE THE
STRIKE! GOOOOOO LANTERNS!**

In bowling and socialism
it is most of all how the
kingpin lays down
with all the others
when the strike is right
for communal victory
there is no Joe Bannana
everybody is one of the bunch.

The Lanterns
worked day and night
to meet competitors:
democrats and republicans,
Mensheviks and Bolsheviks,
Stalinists and Leninists,
males and females,
Milwaukee and Merrill,
seen and unseen,
conditioning and non-conditioning.

On the day of finals
Claire noticed something
while giving her grandpa
some last minute tips
on his hook shot:

(As Claire said in her visionary book, *Alternative Origins of Species*, **"There are no accidents, only precedents for things you think you can't change, but can. ...** No better test of viewpoints concerning revolution exists than the verification of how each worked out during the revolution itself, just as a system of swimming is best tested when a swimmer jumps into the water, or a system of genes is tested through a revolutionary leap, or when a bowler believes and wheels a perfect strike."

What Claire noticed:
on every Merrill bowling shirt
the Lantern was filled
with a numinous light.

Next day she smiled
as she read the front page
of the *Merrill Star*,
glowing from top to bottom:

**MERRILL LANTERNS STATE BOWLING CHAMPIONS
SWEEP VICTORY OVER MILWAUKEE KEGS
STRIKE STRANGELY UNPRECEDENTED.**

Unintended Sutras

MEMORY PALACE

17

The Disappearance of Snow Angels

CLAIRE VOYANT'S PAPYRUS FRAGMENTS, "MY MOTHER," EDITED OUT OF "ALTERNATIVE ORIGINS OF SPECIES"

She was laying down,
flapping her arms in the snow;
the usual stars were overhead:
hunters and hunted,
bows and Eros, bears and belts,
and endless streams of ecliptics,
constellations from the sky's histories of wild shapes.

It seemed—more than now, then—
since light pollution eradicated
the conjunction of stars and navigation—
not from the dome above,
but from our memories of seeing the whole picture,
not fragments and bleed-throughs
from something distant,
dead things brought alive by shimmering light,
spreading through time into future's eyes.

She was laying down,
face-up in the snow,
and nobody knew what she saw that night,
with a billion stars forming a curveball;
she was used to that game—uncertainty—
but it was different this night,
in the snow, some strange desperation,
or maybe a faith few can know,
of liberation and continuation,
interrupted by mortality.

"For a moment we are snow angels.
For a moment we are snow—
human doilies
frozen lace,
until we melt to flesh
and must leave this place."

She stood up and walked out of the house,
out on the four babies who would blame her—
not so much for the betrayal,
but for leaving them without warning.

Everybody sees a different kind of Milky Way,
and she saw a great white path
that carried her to a stop,
to a place where she could belong forever,
become something immortalized.

None of us could understand.
Sure, the signs were there,
like blood red moons and
strange celebrations of courage.

"For a moment we are snow angels.
For a moment we are snow—
human doilies
frozen lace,
until we melt to flesh
and must leave this place."

She was no angel. Nobody is.
She was like those giant nebula
that shoot out beams of matter
at light speed—a force that pulls
matter inward, then propels it outward
to form something new,
like the streams of high-energy particles
that race from the heart of a galaxy.
All I can say is that jets on this scale
effect the evolution of the clusters they reside in,
the family they live with.

Maybe it is not right to remember these things—
our mothers, our births,
accretion and loss, abandonment,
the light we will someday become
to form new species,
or the laws of strengthening, of rapid spinning.
Laws of humans becoming angels
and angels becoming human,
laws of black holes and event horizons,
dynamic and fragile systems,
stars forming and dying—
so many embedded nurseries.
Explosion, collapse: beating wings falling to Earth

It could be that we
are opaque to invisible light;
it could be that we are really snow angels,
giant objects with cores that are slowly colliding
with infinity's celestial remembrance
or it could be
we are flesh strung on bones
impacted by sadness so deep
it denies expression
even in chanted words
and distant metaphors

Unintended Sutras

MEMORY PALACE

18

Seven-Layer Salad

HISTORY REMEMBERED BY
CASSANDRA SHAURS,
ASIAN STUDIES MAJOR,
DAUGHTER OF C. VOYANT.

"The whole body is like a mouth hung is space; without question of east, west, south, or north winds, it equally tells others of wisdom. Drop after drop freezes."

—Shobogenzo, Zen Essays by Dogen

I always wondered about the statement, "drop after drop freezes."
You mean like water freezes?
You mean a phase transition?
One day it hit me—not just the idea of wisdom,
but wisdom as water, and why wisdom traditions
are so deeply imbedded in Midwest potlucks, picnics, barbecues.
I became enamoured of the thought:
that drop after drop could freeze,
suspend itself cryogenically,
and thaw when future generations were ready
to receive drips, layered architecture of all kinds of food,
capsules to feed all kinds of situations,
diverse chemistry, engineering,
evolution and presentation in a nutshell.

Let's talk about iceberg lettuce:

The earliest depiction of lettuce is in the carvings at the temple of Senussret I at Karnak, where he offers milk to the god Min, to whom lettuce was sacred. Lettuce was considered an aphrodisiac in Ancient Egypt, and appears in *The Contendings of Horus and Seth*. Greek physicians later thought lettuce could act as a sleep-inducing agent—in fact the phrase "you made your bed now you have to lie in it" is an allusion dating back to the cultivation of lettuce beds and their seductive powers of sleep. The Romans cultivated lettuce as well, and it eventually made its way to the Papal Courts at Avignon, France. Christopher Columbus introduced lettuce to the New World, and Marquette and Joliette brought it from France down the Mississippi, to Wisconsin and Minnesota, and all the way down south to New Orleans.

Merrill took it on quite easily, readily;
the Green Lantern serves it up every Friday night
as an alternative to coleslaw.

It seemed right and just that it be
the core ingredient for a seven-layer salad—
a salad that worked its way into the hearts and minds
of folks not only from Wisconsin and Minnesota,
but all the way down South, taking on peas and bacon,
variations of cheeses, morphing and mutating,
adapted by many restaurant chefs.
A good seven-layer salad on the menu
became known as "stacking the deck."

A seven-layer salad is best served in a glass bowl
so you can observe the layers and intricacies of design.

Claire Voyant says that by putting it in glass,
feeding becomes a whole new game, with new physics.
Since the observer and the observed merge,
the secrecy of layering leftovers is emancipated—
though mayonnaise remains
in the mix like the tusk of a woolly mammoth,
a key piece in the puzzle of pre-history.
During the ice ages, iceberg lettuce was grown in caves.

She writes a lot about this in her book,
Alternative Origins of Species:
how we cook DNA is similar to how we grow things,
reorient recipes that emerge from the same stem cell,
particular codes embedded in the seven layer salads.

Claire's my mom, and she has always been on the fringes,
embarrassingly so. Ever since I was a kid
she gave me lectures on the number seven,
said it was sacred and appeared in all times and cultures:
seven days of creation, seven days in a week,
seven notes in a musical scale, seven-up, seven-card stud,
seven gates of heaven in Revelations, seven sacraments,
seven deadly sins (till we lowered the baseline)
seven original planets (till we got better optics),
seven stars in the Pleiades (not counting marauders), and her favorite,
seven chakras (not including the ones that go out into space)—
chakras, right next to the seven-layer salad,
the spinning energy vortices in the body,
counterpart to the physical and the manifest,
the subtle layering of the wheel any party turns on.

Seven Layer Salad:

ORIGIN:

Place of Origin: United States

Region or State: Merrill, Wisconsin

Secondary Regions or States:

Minnesota and the Southern United States

DISH DETAILS:

Course Served: Salad

Serving Temperature: Cold

Main Ingredients: ICEBERG LETTUCE, tomatoes, cucumbers, onions, sweet peas (south), hard-boiled eggs, sharp cheddar cheese, bacon bits

Note: Traditional seven layer salads are smothered with coatings of mayonnaise or sour cream and this outrageous act has helped to give salads a controversial name in health arenas.

My mom says that the reason people love
a well-intentioned seven layer salad
is that somewhere in the recesses of their consciousness
they see possibilities of building—
dreams that they can see in the layers of time,
restrictions they have chosen by picking off the top,
or not daring to dig down and excavate the bottom
where the real treasures are. They ignore the stuff that fell
between the layers, or to the bottom, through gravity and density.
The highs and lows are what my mom has a propensity for.

My kind of stepdad, Lance Mainard—who has spent his
life through virtue of his career at the bottom layers—
says that where we dwell, within or between the layers
is a matter of choice and precedence.
Human potential can embrace all seven layers or get stuck in one,
but true beauty and learning and taste are in between the layers,
where so much happens in the interface.
Maybe that is the interface where drop after drop freezes,
where icebergs form and submerge, and lettuce
can re-imagine itself from Egypt into the pyramids of Wisconsin
and the mysteries of Merrill, where our minds and mouths
can discover a brave new multi-layered world
or just **hang**
in
space.

Unintended Sutras

MEMORY PALACE

19

What's Out There is In Here

THOUGHTS OF GETTING ON THE BOAT BY LANCE MAINARD, THIRD GENERATION POLICE OFFICER, MERRILL, WI.

It's true that people are suffering.
Every day I see systems emerging
that are not hospitable for human or non-human survival.
Here in Merrill, we are a farming community
pushed beyond thresholds into new operating systems,
big industry and corporate pirates have infiltrated
the fabric of cultural, economic, and social institutions—
same as everywhere, but we have to look past that to the bigger web.

We have rainwater in our veins and saltwater in our cells,
trillions of bacteria in our guts,
seven hundred species in our mouths alone;
we are linked to Earth's magnetic field through our hearts
and dance floors. The environment is not out there,
it is in here, in us, every environment, **every challenge.**

Searching for new worldviews is not easy.
Interrelationships are not easy; interdependence is not easy.
We are emptiness and do not exist without these.

We are empty unless we are part of something.
Environments without discrete boundaries
push us into new levels of organization;
ultimately it is for us to choose to bias one level or another—
but if we ignore the others we may be unprepared for what unfolds.

Every day I pray for some new ethical imperative
to help all of us secure lives of quality.
Some ethical mutation, a new biological, psychological wisdom
that will help us decide how to live on the Earth
and with each other—how to live with ourselves
so our essences avoid extinction, so as not to kill the seed
or mutate it beyond recognition like Monsanto.
Life is a giant bee hive, swarming in us and around us;
we are not floating, but embedded in the hive.
If we do not cultivate the true seed,
the honeycomb that sustains us, that is us,
we will miss the boat; our perspectives will be a cul-du-sac.

We are always burdened with our ingrained views.
As a police officer I have many—ethnicity, gender,
socio-economics. The more I think of interrelationships,
the more I disarm my old patterns of thought,
the more I change and rewrite my own story,
the more I understand the beauty and fragility
of all systems, and search frantically
to find cenotes, secret spaces and passages within myself,
and let go of the grief I feel for losses not my own.

We have rainwater in our veins and saltwater in our cells,
trillions of bacteria in our guts,
seven hundred species in our mouths alone.
We are the oceans we **vanish into.**

The more I feel proportion, harmony, rhythm,
the more capable I feel of appreciating beauty.
I am a living tipping point of phase transitions,
melting down to deeper and deeper truths
that I see in Nature, human nature, the nature of everything—
even mind-made things and systems,
artificial differences and proportions.
When I try to touch my tears, they freeze.
I wait for the courage to carve ice sculptures
that will announce a change—
a new world to help me reclaim the love I am losing,
find the anger to fight for the enigma,
and not miss the boat.

Life is when we ride in a boat,
understand the operations: sails, rudders, poles—
the boat carries us and we carry the boat.
We make the boat. The boat becomes all the workings.
The boat is our world; the boat is the sky, the water, the shore;
it is all of Earth and space and time.
It is me and all of the circumstances that are not the boat
and I am living and breathing,
and something is causing me to live with all of it.

We have rainwater in our veins and saltwater in our cells
trillions of bacteria in our guts,
seven hundred species in our mouths alone
we are linked to Earth's magnetic field through our hearts
and dance floors. The environment is not out there,
it is in here, in us, every environment, every challenge.
We foster **this totality.**

I have to practice flowing from reality.
If I don't do that—live and flow—
there is no way I can ever merge with any reality.
This is the issue at hand, and my participation
will turn this long river into butter.

Through this, vision and understanding appear to me
in a Midwest town where I am bound for extinction,
feeling my way for a corner of the galaxy
that is in the **palm of my hand pressed to the rudder.**

Unintended Sutras

20

MEMORY PALACE

Understanding the Whey

TEACHINGS OF ANCESTOR CHU, MERRILL MYSTIC AND ARTIFACT.

There is no inside or outside,
no doing or not doing,
no stepping inward or outward—
only finding the gate of the vast energy.
This is the true way:
the nature of things is the teacher,
which is you and ten million things.

People eat food,
especially Friday night at the Green Lantern.
But the food also eats people,
and it eats the Green Lantern too.
Flowers bloom and leaves fall,
fish spawn and are caught,
bowling balls race down the alley
and yield a strike,
or the strike propels movement
where there was stasis,
claims the entire event.
People from the past visit the future
and beings from the future work in factories,

But it is all only thought
that has fallen out within a pattern—
the thought of the nature of things.

What is a cow?
What does a cow know? See? Feel?
It is as holy as the hands that feed it,
as holy as the hands that squeeze it.
Does it realize the nature of things?
Or does it leave the nature of things
to the hands and hooves that imprint time?

Cows produce milk which is the nature of things.
Milk is food and life and cheese,
it is the origination of our galaxy,
it is absorbed and absorbing—
the nature of things, the infinite capacity
of time to nourish us in the present.
The unexpected features of the nature of things
find us at the quantum level—
this comes from understanding the whey.

Did you know that whey is milk plasma?
Whey is liquid remaining after milk
has been curdled and strained.
This is the nature of things—
the nature of plasma in physics is unique,
responding to electromagnetic fields
much like the heart.
Plasma is unlike solids or liquids or gases,
it is a distinct state of matter
without shape or volume (unlike Merrill hair-dos).
It is the nature of things. It is the nature of stars.

The nature of all of us is to create lightening,
to interact with fields, to recognize our plasma state,
our arcs and our filamentation, our fractal forms,
shocks and layers, our rapidly-changing potential,
sharp gradients and velocities,
inductive capacity that will help us accelerate
into new currents and exchanges,
things we could never have dreamed
about the nature of things.

These are the places where thoughts stir,
where universes are formed.
These are the reasons the hundreds of plants
have flowers and fruits.
Earth, water, fire, metal, space, trees—
all have flowers and fruits that are watered by milk.
We cannot talk about flowers in the sky,
or lotuses on land, without understanding the whey.
When we understand the nature of things,
when we understand the whey,
the sky is luminous, the earth is solid,
and humans are fully conscious.

One day at Deer Park Monastery in Oregon, Wisconsin
my student Miss Voyant commented,
"Who names a city after a state where you achieve another state?
Who names a monastery after an animal hunted in Wisconsin?"
We sat silently and heard the wind blow
through bells in the garden. Claire found that the bells
were recycled propane tanks, forged and plasma cut
with cedar tongues to bounce off the insides
and create infinite harmonics.
I asked her seriously and earnestly,
"Is the wind ringing, or the bell ringing?"
She replied:

“Ancestor Chu,

it is not the

wind ringing or the bell ringing;

it is our minds ringing.”

Unintended Sutras

MEMORY PALACE

21

Cenote

I am away in Mexico writing about memory palaces:
things we construct in our heads, clues, metaphors,
pieces of string, breadcrumbs to spark a deeper remembrance
of the cathedrals built inside us by people and things
we meet up with, places we travel.

Smells, dreams, lines, circles, events right in front of us,
or in remote recesses that we put away,
rush through the colander of brain's awareness;
some stay and some sift, like water washing up
the sand and rocks in the mind of the sea
to help reveal the secret places.

Yesterday, I visited a cenote:
the Mayans here in the Yucatan found places
they named dzonots, sacred holes; the Spanish call them cenotes,
locations to find cool fresh water
and gain entrance to the underworld of the spirit,
formed when rainwater carved tunnels
and ceilings collapsed, opening up caves to the surface.

Cenotes link to cave systems that interconnect
to even deeper subterranean water,
like the sea caves in Wisconsin
and the ones we pry open ourselves though our own cataclysms,
joining things that had no way to link up—
not because they shouldn't, but because they couldn't.
Our brains and spirits need that cool fresh water
running through, creating entrance to the palaces
that have forgotten us.

Epilogue

"All living creatures of whatever class,
whether hatched from eggs or born from gas,
from Midwest wombs to Egyptian tombs,
through selective emergence
or genetic convergence,
from birds' north migration
to souls' transportation—

form or without form,
thinking or without thinking,
we attain liberation by breaking the norm
and sometimes drinking.

That's why a sutra can be unintended,
upheaving the ones less comprehended.
Farmers, tanners, and marharishis
enfold the patterns of alternative species;
the train's not leaving any station
till bodhisattvas join into one big nation.
god's face is in the silver cup,
in big gold spoons and runners up."

—C. Voyant

Donna Carey, LAc

Donna Carey is an author, poet, licensed acupuncturist, herbalist, sound healer, and educator. She is co-author of *Acutonics From Galaxies to Cells, Planetary Science, Harmony, and Medicine*, and *Acutonics: There's No Place Like Ohm, Sound Healing, Oriental Medicine, and the Cosmic Mysteries*, she has also authored numerous articles that have appeared in leading journals. Donna is a co-founder of the Kairos Institute of Sound Healing, creators of the Acutonics® Healing System. Driven by the desire to create a sustainable future, Donna is also engaged in experiments in the intentional use of sound vibration to enhance agricultural production, she manages extensive gardens, including a 33-foot geodesic growing dome, and is engaged in forest stewardship programs.